Follow me

Rose Michael

WRITTEN BY ROSE MICHAEL

Follow me

Daily Words from God

TATE PUBLISHING
AND ENTERPRISES, LLC

Published by Tate Publishing & Enterprises, LLC
127 E. Trade Center Terrace | Mustang, Oklahoma 73064 USA
1.888.361.9473 | www.tatepublishing.com

Tate Publishing is committed to excellence in the publishing industry. The company reflects the philosophy established by the founders, based on Psalm 68:11,
"The Lord gave the word and great was the company of those who published it."

Published in the United States of America

ISBN: 978-1-61346-440-3
1. Religion / Christian Life / Spiritual Growth
2. Religion / Christian Life / Inspirational
11.09.07

Acknowledgments

There are several people I want to thank. First and foremost, thank you, Lord, for loving me so unconditionally, for speaking to me, certainly not because I am worthy or deserving, but because you chose me to hear and write these words. In my good days and bad, you were always so faithful to me. When I would run to you or away from you, you were still always there. Through all of life's trials, I never lost sight of one thing, and that is how much you love me. I pray all of your children can get ahold of that one truth. It will get them through anything in life.

I want to thank my children, Christian and Jami, for making being a parent worthwhile. I am so proud of you both and want you to know you are both the jewels in my crown. I am so aware of your unconditional love for me and how much you honor me in your words and actions. I love you both so much.

I want to thank Jamye Lane, a new friend God has brought into my life, who has truly become an amazing sister to me. Without her encouragement and support, this book would probably still be sitting in a drawer. Thank you for believing in me. Your transparency and honesty is so refreshing.

Donna Miller, thank you for putting this manuscript into a format to be published. What a willing vessel you are to help someone you didn't even know. Your reward is coming. And it will be better than anything man can ever give.

How I love you. Come; follow me, and I shall show you things yet unseen. For I, the Lord, look down and choose to whom I will reveal my secrets to and who will carry out my work. For it is in these last days, my Spirit will be poured out, and I ask my people to follow me.

Table of Contents

Introduction

I am a simple person to the world. Though I have no degrees or diplomas to put beside my name, I do have the Word of God that says,

> The Lord God has given me the tongue of the learned, that I should know how to speak a word in season to him who is weary. He awakens me morning by morning, he awakens my ear to hear as the learned.
>
> Isaiah 50:4

My desire is not to be known, but for Him to be known.

Follow Me was written during a time in my life when everything around me was falling apart. What should have been the most crippling of times for me became a time of pressing into my Lord and hearing His voice in such a profound way that it forever changed my life. I do not claim *Follow Me* to be the Word of God, but rather words whispered into my ears, with a message to all of us. God is calling His body together, to become one—whole and complete. Each of us answering His call and taking our positions he has prepared us for.

Do you know where you fit into the body? Do you know your gifts and calling? If you do, *Follow Me* will challenge you to press in even more to hear His voice more clearly and live with a purpose. If you are not sure or you are thinking, I have never even heard His voice, then *Follow Me* will exhort you, encourage you, and teach you through prayer and meditating on the Word of God to learn to be still and hear that still small voice.

I recently had a vision from the Lord. I saw heaven open up, and the throne of God was before me. I noticed the throne was empty, and I said, "Lord, where are you?" I saw before me a man on a white horse, dressed in white, with a sword in His hand. I heard Him say, "I am standing ready, waiting for my army to gather, for I am calling them from all corners of the earth. They are taking their places, for I have called them for such a time as this." And I saw angels from all corners of the earth, blowing trumpets and saying, "The time is now, he is calling." And I saw people, too many to count, coming from every corner of the earth. They were dropping everything, leaving behind anyone who would not follow. They were holding onto nothing, only answering the one who was calling. For they were likened to the bridesmaids, ready with their lamps full, ready to lay down everything and follow him who called out, "Follow me."

My heart's cry is that as you read and meditate on the words written on these pages, you will let go of anything holding you back from following Him; that you will take your position in the body of Christ and let Him use us together as one body. Just as each part of our body connects to the whole body so that it can function correctly, so too we function the same way in Christ's body. Each part is as important as the other. So humbly submit to one another, lifting each other up in love and prayer: "For we are His workmanship, created in Christ Jesus for good works, which God prepared beforehand that we should walk in them" (Ephesians 2:10).

May you hear his voice as you follow Him.

The Calling

When He had called the people to Himself, with His disciples also, He said to them, "Whoever desires to come after me, let him deny himself, and take up his cross, and follow me."

Mark 8:34

There is only one road to follow. There is only one choice to make. If you follow me, I am the road, and I am that choice. How I desire you to follow me. For in following me, you shall find out why I created you and why I named you and called you out of darkness. Do not tie yourself to this world, for it is bondage. It holds you back and keeps you from me. My desire is to free you and bring you into full knowledge of my plans for you. If you will call out my name, and take that first step, I will be by your side. I will lead the way, and light the path, if you will only follow me.

Choose for yourselves this day whom you will serve.

Joshua 24:15

Your word is a lamp to my feet and a light to my path.

Psalm 119:105

Do you not know how much I desire to be with you? Do you not know my heart breaks because our communion has been broken? Will you not come to sit still awhile and listen to me? For you know my voice, but do not hear me calling, because of your constant running to and fro. I am calling an army—a people who will go where I send them. Will you answer my calling to you? For I need you in my army; there are many wars to fight, and I need to equip you before you face the battles. If you will only sit at my feet, I will begin to dress you in my armor I have made just for you. For each warrior will be clothed in a handmade garment, prepared by my hand. Some will be dressed in strength, some in boldness, others in meekness, and some in faith. Each will be equipped for what I commission them to do. There is not much time left to answer me, for I need you now. Come follow me, now—do not be left behind! Come sit, and hear what I have for you, and know that I love you and desire to fellowship with you. Hurry, my little ones, come as you are, and I shall make you ready for battle. Come; follow me.

My sheep hear My voice, and I know them,
and they follow Me.

John 10:27

Put on the whole armor of God, that you may
be able to stand against the wiles of the devil.

Ephesians 6:11

Shoulder to shoulder, I line you up, dressed and ready for battle; I am your shield. Do not be afraid, for you have been equipped and trained. Listen to my voice, for instructions shall come soon. Be ready and prepared to obey, as I give out the commands. Oh, how I have longed for this day! How I am so ready to lead my army, for I am King of Kings and Lord of Lords. I am the Lion of Judah. I am the Beginning and the End. Blow the trumpets, sound the alarm, for I am coming for a pure, holy, and unblemished people. You are my people, so turn your ear to hear, open your eyes to see, and come follow me.

Our soul waits for the Lord; He is our help
and our shield.

Psalm 33:20

I am the Alpha and the Omega, the Beginning
and the End, the First and the Last.

Revelations 22:13

Listen! Can you not hear the earth rejoice? Even the rocks cry out, because they know I am returning soon. You will know neither the day, nor the hour, but I tell you it is soon. Oh, my people, tarry no longer with the world, but quickly come and learn from me. Listen to my voice daily, and learn to recognize it, as a sheep knows the shepherd's voice. For I tell you, in these last days, many will call out in my name, and only my sheep who have sat at my feet shall know if it is my voice that calls or those who have been planted by the deceiver. Make haste, my children, for time is drawing near. Come, follow me.

But He answered and said to them, "I tell you that if these should keep silent, the stones would immediately cry out."

Luke 19:40

And when he brings out his own sheep, he goes before them; and the sheep follow him, for they know his voice. Yet they will by no means follow a stranger, but will flee from him, for they do not know the voice of strangers.

John 10:4–5

Be alert! Stay on guard. Now is not the time to sleep. Wake up, oh people, stir from your apathy. Take up your armor and prepare yourself for the battle coming. I will lead the way. I am the captain but many of you have been chosen to lead by my side. Have your lamps full. Don't be caught low on oil; for I am coming soon and you must be ready when I call.

Purify yourselves. Become a holy people. For I will burn up what is not holy in you when I come to judge. Make sure what is in you is not of wood and straw, for if it is, it will be burned. Come to me with contrite and repentant hearts and I will fill it with a new wine. I will fill it with the things of God that will stand the proof of fire. And you shall be cleansed and made holy; set apart as you follow Me.

Because it is written, "Be holy for I am holy."
1 Peter 1:16

Now if anyone builds on this foundation with gold, silver, precious stones, wood, hay, straw, each one's work will become clear; for the Day will declare it, because it will be revealed by fire; and the fire will test each one's work, of what sort it is. If anyone's work which he has built on it endures, he will receive a reward. If anyone's work is burned, he will suffer loss; but he himself will be saved, yet so as through fire.
1 Corinthians 3:12–15

Oh, how the time is short. Gather together, my children, and listen to my words, for I am beginning to call each of you by name. As you hear your name, come—do not hesitate to answer, for there is not much time. You shall come, one by one, in every city, in every state. For there is a number I am looking for, and my army shall be great. My army will be victorious. My army will be those who have answered their name and have come to hear the commands, for I shall lead my army, and my people shall follow me.

To him the doorkeeper opens, and the sheep hear His voice; and He calls His own sheep by name and leads them out.

John 10:3

The Lord gives voice before His army, for His camp is very great.

Joel 2:11

My faithful ones, how I love you. You have walked through the fires of tribulation and come out purified and holy. For you kept your eyes on me, and your tongues praised my name. When you did not see the light, you praised my name. When you had no hope of the trials ever ending, you praised my name. When it seemed darkness was all around you, still you praised my name. My people, I call you my faithful ones because you have let me prove you.

It is time for the fires of trial to lift from my people, and blessings shall be poured out upon you. It is time I lift my people up, and the world shall see that those who served me shall be exalted by their Lord. I shall bring to my people wealth that will astound those around you. I shall bring honor and success and position to those who have been faithful to me. No longer shall my people be downtrodden and defeated, but victorious and strong. My people shall make ready, the way for my return, triumphant and joyous, ever ready to follow me.

We also glory in tribulations, knowing that tribulation produces perseverance, and perseverance, character, and character, hope.

Romans 5:3

The Lord will establish you as a holy people to Himself... then all peoples of the earth shall see that you are called by the name of the Lord.

Deuteronomy 28:9

Oh, my people, follow me. For I speak with clarity to those who will listen. But you must be still before me, for I speak in that still, small voice. I will not shout at you to override your own voice. You must learn to be quiet so you can hear me. There is no hidden secret in hearing me; only that you sit before me in quietness. I ask this of you so that my Spirit can speak to you and teach you all that you need to know. In these last days, I need my people ready to listen and ready to obey. Hasten to me as little children, eager to learn and to carry out the orders of the Father. My Spirit is ready to be poured out in you, if you will only follow me.

You shall walk after the Lord your God and fear Him, and keep His commandments and obey.

Deuteronomy 13:4

And it shall come to pass in the last days, says God, that I will pour out My spirit on all flesh.

Acts 2:17

It is real! It is possible to hear the voice of the Lord speaking to your spirit. There is a godly balance in hearing from the Lord. If you are not reading the Word of God and rely only on what you hear, then you are deceived. If you read the Word of God, but do not seek relationship and learn My voice, then you are in the law. I say My sheep know my voice. How can you know My voice if you do not believe you can hear Me? Quietly come to me. Read My written word. Meditate on it and listen as you rest quietly before Me. You will hear Me. The more you come the clearer you will hear. Always take what you hear to the written Word. It is your safety net. It is the truth and will not lie. If what you hear does not line up with the Word, then dismiss it. Oh, how I delight in teaching you to Follow Me.

The voice of the Lord is powerful; the voice of the Lord is full of majesty.

Psalm 29:4

So then faith comes by hearing, and hearing by the word of God.

Romans 10:17

How I delight in the holiness of my people. I am pleased with my faithful ones. You have overcome and stand before me, ready to receive the fruits of your labor, for I am the giver of all things, and I choose whom I bless. Oh, my children, prepare for my blessings. Though I only ask for a tenth, I give back a hundredfold. For, my children, you have been faithful and obedient to my will. You have walked in my statutes and in righteousness. For my name's sake, you have been ridiculed and mocked. But, I, the Lord your God, shall lift you up and shall call you mine before all the world because you have followed me.

A faithful man will abound with blessings.

Proverbs 28:20

And he who overcomes, and keeps My works until the end, to him I will give power over the nations.

Revelation 2:26

My children, I shall teach you to walk a deeper walk with me. You will learn to hold your arms out in forgiveness toward one another, even as I held my arms out toward you as I died on the cross. It is my desire for my children to learn this and walk in it. As you sit quietly in my presence, you will not only hear me; you will become my nature. For I am the branch, and you are the vines, and as the branch produces much fruit, so do the vines. Empty yourselves of worldly things, and I shall fill you with spiritual things, for a person cannot serve two masters, nor can you put new wine in an old skin. For what I have to give you is new and fresh and cannot be put into the old skin. But I shall create a new skin in you, if you will only lay down your old skin and follow me.

For if you forgive men their trespasses, your heavenly Father will also forgive you.

Matthew 6:14

And no one puts new wine into old wineskins; or else the new wine bursts the wineskins, the wine is spilled, and the wineskins are ruined. But new wine must be put into new wineskins.

Mark 2:22

Oh, my beloved people, will you not hasten unto me? For I am ready to send you out into the fields. For the harvest is ready, but my laborers so few. There is much work ahead for you, but it will be a labor that produces so much fruit. It will be a work you shall take joy in. Come sit, and I will pour out my Spirit upon you, my children, for my desires will become your desires, and the longings of my heart shall become my people's longings. As you sit at my feet, so shall you take on the nature of your God. Learn to wait upon me, and I shall send you out, anointed and bold. Learn to listen, for my words will bring you wisdom. Learn to obey, and I shall lift you to higher places. As eagles soar high above in splendor and beauty, so too shall you, my people, as you learn to follow me.

Then He said to them, "The harvest truly is great, but the laborers are few; therefore pray the Lord of the harvest to send out laborers into His harvest."

Luke 10:2

As newborn babes desire the pure milk of the word, that you may grow thereby.

1 Peter 2:2

My children, come listen to me. For it is time to take you from the milk and give to you solid food. For though I desire your hearts to come to me as little children, I desire your spirit to grow and mature into adulthood. Time is so short. Hasten to me, and eat the food I have prepared for you. As you eat, you will learn to lay down everything and follow me.

When I was a child, I spoke as a child ... but when I became a man, I put away childish things.

1 Corinthians 13:11

My people, how I long to talk to you day and night, to show you the depth of my love, to make you understand why I died for you, to tell you I want you just as you are. There is nothing you can do to make yourself ready for me, for it is my grace that brings you into fellowship with me. It is my grace that covers your sins and brings you to the throne. It is my love for you that desires you, just as you are, blemishes and all. It is my love that will take away those blemishes, as you come and follow me.

But God demonstrates His own love toward us, in that while we were still sinners, Christ died for us.

Romans 5:8

I have not come to call the righteous, but sinners to repentance.

Luke 5:32

You are to rely on Me. Trust Me. Do not live your life whirling around another, letting their moods control you. Learn to stabilize yourself even in the worst of storms. How is that possible? By trusting Me!

Depend on Me! I am your source. I am your rock on which you stand.

When you make Me your foundation, you will not fall. I created you to need each other but not to be needy of one another. When that occurs, you become unbalanced in your thinking and emotions. When you turn to Me to fill the needs of your heart, you will become whole and complete. Not only will you stay free, you will enable the others in your life to become healthy too.

Come run to the Living Water, and I will fill your heart with the things that count for good. I will fill you with an overflow that will spill onto others and forever change you and the ones around you. I Am that I Am. I Am your all in all. Depend on Me as you learn to trust and follow Me.

He who believes in Me, as the Scripture has said, out of his heart will flow rivers of living water.

John 7:38

The Lord is my rock and my fortress and my deliverer.

Psalm 18:2

Come, all who are ready to take up your cross, and follow me. It is time to lose your life to me so that you may save it. It is time to answer me, for I have called your name, and I ask you to lay down your things and follow me. My beloved people, it is time to be either hot or cold, but no longer lukewarm, for I am calling together my people—my army. I have already assigned many positions to those who, so long ago, heard my voice and followed me. My desire is for you to come to me and follow, but you, my people, must make that choice. I will only ask, I will not choose for you.

My longing is for every one of my children to choose life over death, freedom over bondage, obedience over rebellion. Take that first step, my child, as you hear me call your name. Lay down your things and follow me.

Then Jesus said to His disciples, "If anyone desires to come after me, let him deny himself, and take up his cross, and follow Me.

Matthew 16:24

For the wages of sin is death, but the gift of God is eternal life in Christ Jesus our Lord.

Romans 6:23

The Teacher

But the Helper, the Holy Spirit, whom the Father will send in my name, He will teach you all things.

John 14:26

My children, you sit at my feet ready to learn—how I delight in your choice to follow me. My greatest desire is that not one of my sheep be left behind.

As you sit quietly before me, I shall begin to teach you and instruct you. There is much to learn, my children, and oh, so little time. But my Spirit shall teach you quickly as you eat the food I have prepared.

I desire first to teach you my voice—that you would recognize it over any other; that you would know it, even when another comes in my name. If you will sit quietly before me and come often, I will speak to you, and you shall hear my voice. For all I ask from you is a willing heart, ready to hear and always obey. For as I walked in obedience to the Father's will on earth, so too, I would ask you to do the same. I ask not for sacrifice, but obedience; for I am not interested in what covers the outward man, but what lies within him. Sacrifice is a garment, worn to show other men. Obedience is an attitude of love toward your Creator. Learn this, my children, and you have learned the first step to follow me.

And when he brings out his own sheep, he goes before them; and the sheep follow him, for they know his voice.

John 10:4

If you are willing and obedient, you shall eat the good of the land.

Isaiah 1:19

There is excitement all around because my people are beginning to see with their spiritual eyes and not their fleshly eyes. The ears of their heart are hearing—not what the world would say, but what my spirit says. For though you are in the world, I say you are not to be of the world. For what you see around you with your fleshly eyes is not real, but what I show you in the spirit is what I desire you to hold fast to, for it is what is real. It is eternal and shall never pass away. For it is written that you do not fight against flesh and blood, but against principalities, against powers, against rulers of the darkness, and against spiritual hosts of wickedness in heavenly places. (See Ephesians 6:12) This is what is real; learn this, as you will follow me.

I do not pray that you should take them out of the world, but that you should keep them from the evil one. They are not of the world, just as I am not of the world.

John 17:15–16

And the world is passing away, and the lust of it; but he who does the will of God abides forever.

1 John 2:17

My beloved people, bend your ear to hear, for I am your teacher and shall make you ready for your calling. Would I call your name and then not speak to you, or instruct you? Surely not! For I am a loving Father who speaks with clarity and direction to his children.

I desire to teach you of the spirit, to bring you into a fuller knowledge of Him and the gifts he brings to you, for there is a mighty power in Him that is to be given to my children. Greater works than these you shall do because of Him, whom I sent you. Receive Him, because it is my desire that you come to know Him. For without the Holy Spirit freely operating in your lives, I cannot bring you into your fullness, for he speaks my words to you, my thoughts and desires to you. He is the third person of the Godhead and is to be worshiped and exalted, for it is written, "But whoever speaks against the Holy Spirit, it will not be forgiven him, either in this age or in the age to come" (Matthew 12:32). For those who speak against me, many never even knew me, but those who speak against the Spirit have known me and walked away. For I say, "Of how much worse punishment, do you suppose, will he be thought worthy, who has trampled the Son of God underfoot, counted the blood of the covenant by which he was sanctified a common thing and insulted the Spirit of grace? (Hebrews 10:29)

My children, guard your hearts and keep them open to learn what my spirit teaches, for he teaches you how to follow me.

> For the Holy Spirit will teach you in that very hour what you ought to say.
>
> Luke 12:12

> But the Helper, the Holy Spirit, whom the Father will send in My name, He will teach you all things.
>
> John 14:26

Not in yourself but in Me. What does that mean? How do you let the power of Me flow through you? The very first thing is knowing that it is not you. You can do nothing apart from Me. I was one with the Father, and He was one with Me. I could do nothing apart from Him while on earth. If I, who am the son of the living God, could do nothing apart from Him, how much more do you need to live in Me? If I needed to pull away to pray daily to My Father, how much more do you? I know the power of the enemy. I know the temptations that are there. I also know the power that lies in you through Me. "You are of God, little children, and have overcome them, because He who is in you is greater than he who is in the world (1 John 4:4). I have sent you someone to live within you that will enable you to overcome. These are truths that My children have not only misunderstood but have not believed. Greater things shall you do! Open your eyes that you may see these truths. Open your ears to hear these truths. Walk in the fullness of what I have given you. Walk in the power of the Holy Spirit. In Me shall you do these things as you follow me.

Then Jesus answered and said to them, "Most assuredly, I say to you, the Son can do nothing of Himself, but what He sees the Father do; for whatever He does, the Son also does in like manner."

John 5:19

These things we also speak, not in words which man's wisdom teaches but which the Holy Spirit teaches, comparing spiritual things with spiritual.

1 Corinthians 2:13

My children, do not let a day go by that you do not sit with me. For I yearn for your fellowship and desire to see you grow. The enemy draws nearer in to my children in these last days, and my need to teach you about your enemy is great. That is the first thing I desire you to know that Satan is the enemy! Do not think that he is not to be taken seriously. He would have you believe that to keep you powerless. But I tell you he is cunning and deceitful and can trap you at anytime, if you do not know him. I tell you to know your enemy and learn his tactics. For I have given you power over your enemy. I have provided the power, through my blood, and give to you the armor to wear. For it is written, "Take up the whole armor of God, that you may be able to withstand in the evil day, and having done all, then stand" (Ephesians 6:13). There is nothing I hold back from you, but freely I give to you. I give to you truth, righteousness, peace, faith, salvation, and the Word. These are your armor to wear and make you ready. Learn, my children, the depth of what I give to you, for this is how you fight your enemy and win. Victory is yours, my children, as you draw closer and learn to follow me.

Lest Satan should take advantage of us; for we are not ignorant of his devices.

2 Corinthians 2:11

Behold, I give you the authority to trample on serpents and scorpions, and over all the power of the enemy, and nothing shall by any means hurt you.

Luke 10:19

My children, watch the eye of a storm. Raging winds and rains are all around, but in the eye there is peace, stillness, safety. I am the eye of your life. I am that peace and safety in the midst of the storms. My blood is the shield of protection from those storms breaking through. My children, learn of the power and authority I gave to you. For my people perish for lack of knowledge. If you will seek my face with all your heart, I shall give to you the keys to unlock the doors to my power and authority that I so long ago gave to you. There is nothing you cannot do in my name, if you bring pure hearts before me; for it is my desire that my people receive unto themselves, all that I gave to them. It is my desire that you walk in the power I sent to you through the Holy Spirit, for I sent Him to abide in you and enable you to walk in authority and power. My beloved people, do you not see that the power dwells within you? Do not go searching for it far away, but look within, for He is the spirit of truth and will show you how to follow me.

And the peace of God, which surpasses all understanding, will guard your hearts and minds through Christ Jesus.

Philippians 4:7

For the kingdom of God is not in word but in power.

1 Corinthians 4:20

My children, look for the signs of my return, for they are all around you. I have not hidden them but have made them clear to see so everyone would turn to me in these last days. For it is written, "The Lord is not willing that any should perish, but that all should come to repentance. But the day of the Lord will come as a thief in the night" (2 Peter 3:9b-10).

My children, it is time to bring in those lost sheep. It is time to lay down your fears and speak out my name. Be bold, my children, and be obedient to my commands. The seeds have been sown, now I ask you to be part of the harvest. If you will seek me, I will show you which direction to go. I will guide you and lead you to your field. My children, follow me.

But the end of all things is at hand; therefore be serious and watchful in your prayers.

1 Peter 4:7

I will instruct you and teach you in the way you should go.

Psalm 32:8

The Surrendered Vessel

But in a great house there are not only vessels of gold and silver, but also of wood and clay, some for honor and some for dishonor. Therefore if anyone cleanses himself from the latter, he will be a vessel for honor, sanctified and useful for the Master, prepared for every good work.

2 Timothy 2:20–21

My children, let me teach you about my love. For I love you beyond what you can ever imagine. There are no boundaries, no conditions, and no limits to my love. My love is pure, holy, and redeeming. My love is free to all my children, if you will only open up your hearts to receive it, for I hold not from you, but you hold from me. Everything I have, I desire my children to have, but only if you surrender to me can you receive all that I have for you. There is so much that you carry, that I have not asked of you. Many of you are so weighed down with your own burdens you cannot even see that I have provided a way for your load to be lightened. Lay down those burdens, my children, for they chain you and keep you in bondage. What I give you is light and will not weigh you down, but bring you into a freedom you have never known. Is it not written, "My yoke is easy and my burden is light?" (Matthew 11:30). "Come to me, all you who labor and are heavy laden, and I will give you rest" (Matthew 11:28). Come, take my yoke, and follow me.

In this is love, not that we loved God, but that He loved us and sent His son to be the propitiation for our sins.

1 John 4:10

For I am persuaded that neither death nor life, nor angels nor principalities nor powers, nor things present nor things to come, nor height nor depth, nor any other created thing, shall be able to separate us from the love of God which is in Christ Jesus our Lord.

Romans 8:38–39

My children, wear me! Don't learn from me and then lay me aside. Let my words go into the very marrow of your bones. Become my nature. Put me on! For it is written, "Put on the Lord Jesus Christ and make no provision for the flesh" (Romans 13:14). As you draw closer to me, as you draw closer to the image of me, you shall become more like me. You will desire to put away the old things and take up the new. It will not be a hard thing to do, but a burning desire to do so, for my spirit who dwells in you will bring you into a holiness and pureness as you draw closer and follow me.

And that you put on the new man which was created according to God, in true righteousness and holiness.

Ephesians. 4:24

Knowing this, that our old man was crucified with Him, that the body of sin might be done away with, that we should no longer be slaves of sin.

Romans 6:6

My beloved people, with open arms I stand before you, ready to receive you and ready to pour out all my gifts to you. Open your arms out to me, my children. For when you do, everything else you hold onto will fall from you. You cannot hold onto me and to the world at the same time. I am your strength, I am your source. I am the very life of you. I yearn for you to understand the depth of my love, though I know you can never fully understand it all. I ache for you to love me, as I love you. Do you not know, my children, I created you for my pleasure? I created you to share everything that is mine with you. Oh, my children receive me, and you shall also receive all that is mine. Let go, my beloved children, of what you hold onto. Reach out your arms and follow me.

For the gifts and the calling of God are irrevocable.

Romans 11:29

The Lord takes pleasure in those who fear Him, in those who hope in His mercy.

Psalm 147:11

Fall on your face before Me and let go of your will and seek My will. Many of you are holding onto things that are not of Me. They are hindering your walk with Me and preventing you from hearing My voice. Some of the things would even seem to be godly, but they are not from Me and I am asking you to lay them down. For what I have for you is the better thing. I am asking you to obey Me. For in obedience you will find your freedom. Let My spirit lead you into the knowledge of the truth. If there be anything in you that is not of Me, let me search it out. Be not afraid, for everything I do and ask of you is because of My great love for you. I see you complete and whole.

So children come to Me, with repentant hearts, willing to be obedient, so I can fill you with new and fresh things as you let go of the old and follow Me.

Search me, O God, and know my heart.

Psalm 139:23

I will instruct you and teach you in the way you should go.

Psalm 32:8

My children, *watch! Listen!* Do not go to sleep, for I may come at any hour. I do not mean physical rest for your body, but spiritual slumber. Do not be lazy in seeking me, but be zealous in your search for me. Come into my presence. Worship me, and give me praise, for these are things which I receive and count as good. In the midst of your worship, there shall I be. For I inhabit the praises of my people. Do not hide behind stone faces and folded arms, for it shows the stubbornness of your heart. But again, I say, open your arms, and lift them to me, for then you become vulnerable and surrender to me, a teachable and yielding spirit. For I do not look for vessels of silver or gold, but for vessels yielding to their creator, ready to be emptied, shaped and molded into what I have created them for. Come, my children, let my spirit teach you how to surrender to me. With open arms, he will lead you to follow me.

Watch therefore, for you do not know when the master of the house is coming—in the evening, at midnight, at the crowing of the rooster, or in the morning—lest, coming suddenly, he find you sleeping. And what I say to you, I say to all: "Watch!"

2 Timothy 2:20–21

Teach me to do your will, For You are my God;

Psalm 143:10

The Bride

Let us be glad and rejoice and give Him glory, for the marriage of the Lamb has come, and His wife has made herself ready.

And to her it was granted to be arrayed in fine linen, clean and bright, for the fine linen is the righteous acts of the saints.

Then he said to me, "Write: Blessed are those who are called to the marriage supper of the Lamb!"

Revelation 19:7–9

Eye has not seen, ear has not heard what I am about to do. I am preparing hearts all over the earth for these last days. Since the days of Moses there will be nothing likened to it. I am moving over all the earth, awakening the hearts of man to the coming of the Lord. So arise, My people. Be ready! For the earth's days are numbered and the harvest is ready. Spread your tent pegs, for the salvation of the Lord is at hand and all that hear will follow Me.

But as it is written: "Eye has not seen, nor ear heard, Nor have entered into the heart of man the things which God has prepared for those who love him."

1 Corinthians 2:9

My people, my children, my bride! I am ready to meet you in the air. My arms open wide, ready to receive you. The marriage supper has been prepared, and it is only a while longer before the marriage of the Lamb begins. My bride has been preparing and making herself ready for her King to ask for her. My heart longs for the day, for I know the beauty of the bride, and that which she gave to become the bride. Be ready, my people, and keep your lamps full. For it is written, "The bridegroom came, and those who were ready went in with him to the wedding; and the door was shut" (Matthew 25:10). Be not those foolish ones who came unprepared and were left behind. Take off your rags of filth, and I shall dress you in fine linen. For it is written, "And to her, *the bride,* it was granted to be arrayed in fine linen, clean and bright, for the fine linen is the righteous acts of the saints" (Revelation 19:8). My Spirit shall lead you into that righteousness and shall make you spotless and holy and without blemish. Come, my children; prepare yourselves to meet me in the air, and follow me.

And the Spirit and the bride say, "Come!" And let him who hears say "Come!" And let him who thirsts come. Whoever desires, let him take the water of life freely.

Revelation 22:17

Come *Follow Me.*